FAJITA FIESTA

by REBECCA REYES

Illustrations by: Dan Glidden
Design by: Flat Lizard Graphics

TABLE OF CONTENTS

"What's It All About"

"FAJITAS" (Pronounced fa HEE tahs) are derived from the Spanish word "faja", meaning belt; "ita" is a suffix of endearment.

"FAJITAS" originated in Mexico and as they crossed the Texas border, they were tenderized and received into the open arms of a soft warm tortilla.

"FAJITAS" also known as the Beef Skirt, can be substituted by the flank steak. The skirt steak is located along the inner rib section of the beef fore quarter short plate.

"FAJITAS" grilled over an open mesquite fire; accompanied by salsas guacamole, sour cream, pico de gallo, arroz, frijoles, and warm tortillas; are rapidly becoming the favorite dish of Mexican food lovers everywhere.

SELECTING "FAJITAS"

Fajitas are becoming more available in our grocery stores. Until recently the fajita was ground or cut into stew meat, now cattle ranchers are specializing in producing a large tender, good fajita.

The Fajita is a long strip of meat, usually measuring 4 to 5 inches in width and 2 to 3 feet in length and can be up to an inch in thickness. The fajita is sold by the pound. Judge approximately ½ to ¾ of a pound per serving. Keep in mind the guests you plan to serve and their appetites.

You will not find the fajita laid out to its full length, but rather is usually folded under on each side. You can have your butcher extend the fajita to show its entire quality. One side of the fajita has more fat. You can have the butcher peel this fat off or we'll show you how to do it at home. Leaving some of the fat on the fajita will add more flavor while cooking. Select your fajita as you would select your other cuts of meat.

Now that you have selected and bought your "Fajitas" turn the page and we'll show you how to prepare them and give you some delicious recipes.

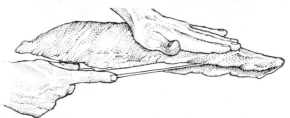

1. Lay fajita lengthwise on a cutting board. With a sharp carving knife, holding the blade parallel with the fajita, begin cutting from the thin wide side. As illustrated.

2. Cut horizontally in half with clean, even strokes, but not all the way through, then open out meat like a butterfly.

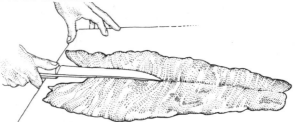

3. Grab excess fat, which should pull away easily, with your fingers. With carving knife cut fat pulling away as you cut, being careful not to cut the meat.

4. With the edge of a carving knife or a meat mallet pound the fajita well for tenderizing.

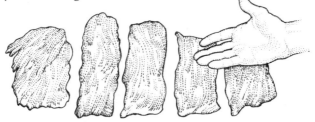

5. Cut crosswise sectioning meat into steaks about 3 to 4 inches wide.

PREPARING "FAJITAS"

Lay the Fajita on your counter and spread it out
to its full length, with the fatty side up. Lift the loose
fat and trim it off carefully with a sharp knife. Some
of the fat will feel and look like the skin of a cooked
tomato and you can usually just peel this off. Do not
remove all the fat so that it may give your fajitas more
flavor. Pound the fajita with the flat side of a butcher
knife or a meat mallet. This breaks down some of the
fibers, and tenderizes the meat.

You can leave the fajita whole and use any marinating method you prefer.

or

You can butterfly the fajita by laying out the fajita
lengthwise, slicing through it almost entirely and spread-
ing apart making a flat piece. Then pound the fajita to
tenderize. This also stretches the portions per serving.

Now that you have selected and prepared the
fajita, let's bring out the full flavor with the perfect
marinade.

MARINADES

JUST FAJITAS

4   *lemons sliced in half*
1   *onion sliced*
dash   *meat tenderizer*
1 tsp.   *salt*
1 tsp.   *pepper*
1 tsp.   *garlic powder*

Prepare fajitas as desired. Place fajita in a marinating pan and sprinkle salt, pepper and garlic powder evenly over meat. Mix in sliced onions. Squeeze lemon juice over meat and mix well; turning meat. Marinade for an hour or more before cooking.

Marinates approximately 4 pounds of fajitas.

FAJITAS ITALIANO   (Italian Fajitas)

3/4 cup   *Italian salad dressing*
1 tsp.   *oregano*
2 tbsp.   *Italian seasons*
1 tsp.   *garlic powder*

Combine all the ingredients, mixing well over fajitas. Marinade for 1 hour or more before cooking.

Marinates 4 pounds fajitas.

FAJITAS BORRACHOS (Drunken Fajitas)

1 tbsp.   *lemon pepper*
1 tsp.   *garlic powder*
1/2 tsp. *salt*
2 tbsp.   *Teriyaki sauce*
1/4 cup   *cooking oil*
1/4 cup   *wine vinegar*
1 can   *beer*
1   *jalapeno, chopped finely*

Sprinkle lemon pepper, garlic powder and salt evenly over meat.
Mix in Teriyaki sauce, cooking oil, vinegar, beer and jalapeno
and work well into meat. Marinade for 1 hour or more before
cooking.

Marinates 4 pounds of fajitas.

FAJITAS DE PINA (Pineapple Fajitas)

1/2 cup   *cooking oil*
1/2 cup   *wine vinegar*
1/2 cup   *onion chopped finely*
1 tsp.   *garlic salt*
1/2 tsp. *pepper*
1 cup   *pineapple juice*

Combine all the ingredients, sprinkling garlic salt and pepper
first and mix well into fajitas. Marinade for 1 hour or more
before cooking. Use remaining marinade for basting.

Marinates 4 pounds of fajitas.

FAJITAS KABOB MARINADE

$1/2$ cup   soy sauce
$1/2$ cup   cooking oil
$1/2$ cup   wine vinegar
$1/2$ tsp.   garlic powder
$1/2$ tsp.   salt
1 tbsp.   lemon pepper
dash   meat tenderizer

Sprinkle garlic powder, salt, lemon pepper and tenderizer over meat. Mix in soy sauce, oil and vinegar. Soak fajitas thoroughly. Refrigerate for 1 hour or more before cooking.

Marinates 4 pounds of fajitas.

NOTAS

BOTANAS

GUACAMOLE (Avocado Dip)

2	ripe avocados
1/4 cup	sour cream
1/2	tomato chopped finely
1/2	onion grated
1/2 tsp.	garlic salt
2 tbsp.	lemon juice

1. Peel avocados and mash well. Add sour cream, tomato, onion, garlic salt and lemon juice; mix well.

2. Garnish with sprinkles of paprika.

CHILE CON QUESO (Chili with Cheese Dip)

1 box	Velveeta cheese
1 8 oz.	can of pet milk
1 10 oz.	can of Rotel tomatoes and green chiles (substitute stewed tomatoes)

1. Using a double boiler at medium temperature, combine cheese and milk; stir until cheese is well melted.

2. Add can of tomatoes and chiles and mix well. For hotter cheese dip add 1 diced jalapeno pepper.

3. As cheese cools it thickens. Serve as a dip or pour over your favorite dish.

APERITIVO DE FRIJOLES   (Bean Dip Appetizer)

2 cups	cooked pinto beans
or	
1 can	refried beans
2 tbsp.	sour cream
2 tsp.	garlic powder
2	jalapeno peppers chopped
4 tbsp.	cooking oil
1 cup	shredded cheddar cheese

1. Heat oil in a skillet and add beans, jalapenos and spices.
    Mash beans well; simmer until beans do not stick to pan.
    Spoon bean mixture into serving dish and mix in sour cream.

2. Garnish with shredded cheese.

SALSA VERDE   (Green Chile Salsa)

8	tomatillos
2 tsp.	chile peppers (serrano or jalapeno)
2 tsp.	garlic powder
1 tsp.	salt
1	large avocado
1/2 cup	milk

1. Remove leafy skin from tomatillos and boil until soft, about
    20 to 30 minutes. Remove and set aside.

2. Boil about 6 chile peppers until soft; about 20 or 30 minutes.
    Place chiles into blender and blend well; remove and pour
    into refrigerated storing container. The blended chile can be
    frozen and defrosted many times.

3. Blend tomatillo, avocado, 2 tbsp. of blended chile, salt,
    garlic, milk and cilantro until well mixed.

4. This salsa can be served warm or chilled. Keep refrigerated
    until needed. Mix well before serving.

SALSA ROJA   (Red Chile Salsa)

6   tomatoes
2 tbsp. blended chiles (See step 2 of Salsa Verde)
1 tsp.   salt
2 tbsp. garlic powder

1. Boil tomatoes about 20 minutes until soft. Skin will appear wrinkled. Dip into cold water and slip skin off.

2. Blend tomatoes, chiles, salt and garlic powder, until well mixed.

3. Serve chilled or warm. Keep refrigerated until needed. Stir before serving.

4. Serve as a dip or over your favorite dish.

TAQUITOS AL CARBON

2 lbs. Fajitas
12   Flour tortillas

1. Prepare and cook fajitas as desired. Slice fajitas into small thin 1 inch slices against the grain.

2. Prepare tortillas or use store bought tortillas. The tortillas should be about 2^1/$_2$ to 3 inches in diameter. Use a cookie press or a small bowl as a marker and cut tortillas. Heat on a griddle and wrap in aluminum foil to keep warm.

3. Fill each tortilla with a spoon full of fajitas, just enough so that the tortilla will fold into a miniature taco.

4. Place taquitos on a serving dish.

FLAUTITAS DE FAJITA

2 lbs.   Fajitas
12   Corn tortillas

1. Prepare and cook fajitas as desired. Chop fajitas finely.

2. Use store bought corn tortillas and cut them into small 3 inch circles. Heat tortillas on a hot griddle.

3. Lay tortilla flat and spoon in fajita mixture and roll tightly. Pin closed with a toothpick.

4. In a frying pan heat about 1 cup cooking oil. Place little tortilla roll into a skillet and fry until crisp and golden brown. Drain on a paper towel.

5. Remove toothpick before serving.

NOTAS

FAJITAS

GRILLED FAJITAS

2   *onions sliced*
4 lbs. *fajitas*

1. Leave fajitas whole or butterfly; pound with a knife or meat mallet to tenderize. Marinade fajitas with your choice of marinade.

2. Cut fajitas into steak size pieces, so that they can go straight from the grill to your plate. Cut the fajita at a sharp diagonal to the grain of the meat.

3. Spread the fajitas on the grill evenly and place slices of onions on top of the fajitas. The grill should be extremely hot.

4. Grill for 5 to 6 minutes on a side for medium rare. About 10 minutes for well done.

5. Serve with hot tortillas, and any accompaniment you prefer. For best results grill over an open mesquite fire.

6. Makes 6 to 8 servings.

FAJITA CHEESE BURRITOS   (Stuffed tortillas rolled and topped with cheese)

2 lbs. *fajitas*
      chile con queso
8   *tortillas*
      sour cream
      guacamole

1. Prepare fajitas as desired and chop into small pieces.

2. Prepare tortillas or use store bought tortillas by heating on a hot griddle.

3. Place fajita mixture into center of tortilla and roll. Place rolled tortilla open side down on a serving dish and cover with Chile con queso. Spoon Guacamole and sour cream over tortilla.

4. Makes 4 servings.

OVEN BROILED FAJITAS

1   onion sliced
2 lbs. fajitas

1. Prepare and marinade fajitas and cut into steak size pieces.

2. Preheat oven to 450F. With a piece of fat trimmed from the
    fajita rub the broiling pan rack. Place the fajita on the rack,
    then place the pan in the broiler. Spread onion slices on top
    of the fajitas. Broil until meat is browned, turning with tongs.
    Cook for about 6 minutes for medium meat or until desired
    degree of doneness.

3. Makes 4 servings.

TOSTADAS DE FAJITA

2 lbs.   fajitas
6   corn tortillas
2 cups   refried beans
         lettuce chopped
         tomatoes diced
2 cups   cheddar cheese grated
2   avocados sliced
         sour cream

1. Prepare fajitas and chop. Prepare tostada shells, refried
    beans, lettuce, tomatoes, cheese and avocados. Set aside.

2. Spread refried beans on fried tortilla, then cover plentifully
    with fajita meat. Top with lettuce, tomatoes, cheese and
    avocados.

3. Garnish with a spoon of sour cream in the middle of the
    tostada.

4. Makes 4 to 6 servings.

FAJITA NACHOS   (Tortilla chips with cheese and fajitas)

1 lb.	fajitas
	tortilla chips
1 cup	refried beans
2 cups	cheddar cheese, shredded
1 cup	chile con queso
2	jalapeno peppers, sliced
5 tbsp.	guacamole
5 tbsp.	sour cream

1. Prepare fajitas and chop into small bite size pieces.

2. Prepare tortilla chips; make your own or use store bought chips. Prepare chile con queso, guacamole and refried beans; set aside.

3. Preheat oven to 350F. Spread refried beans on each tortilla chip. Place chips on an oven proof plate, covering plate completely. Sprinkle shredded cheddar cheese generously over beans. Place in the oven and bake for about 5 minutes or until cheese has melted.

4. Remove plate from oven and spread fajita meat evenly over melted cheese, so that each chip has a nice helping of meat. Pour chile con queso over meat and top with sliced jalapenos and spoons of guacamole and sour cream.

5. Serve with fresh chips.

FAJITA FLAUTAS (Flute-shaped Tacos)

2 lbs. fajitas
12   corn tortillas
1 cup cooking oil
*   toothpicks*

1. Prepare fajitas as desired. Fajita flautas are exceptionally great stuffed with Fajitas Ranchero. Or you can just chop your fajitas finely for stuffing.

2. Soften tortillas over warm griddle. Before heating corn tortillas dampen with water. (They soften quicker this way.)

3. Lay tortilla flat and spoon in fajita mixture and roll tightly. Pin closed with a toothpick.

4. In a 12 inch skillet heat oil. Place tortilla roll into skillet and fry until crisp and golden brown. Drain on paper towel.

5. Remove toothpick before serving. Serve with a spoon of guacamole and one of sour cream on top of the tortilla roll.

6. Makes 6 servings.

PAN FRIED FAJITAS

1   onion sliced
2 lbs. Fajitas
3 tbsp. cooking oil

1. Follow step 1 and 2 from the grilled fajitas.

2. In a frying skillet, over moderate temperature, brown meat in oil until done, turning occasionally. When turning the meat, use tongs so that the meat will not be pierced and the juices lost. Place onion over fajitas while frying.

3. Do not cover meat. Fry for 10 to 15 minutes for medium meat.

4. Makes 4 servings.

FAJITAS RANCHERO (Ranch Style Fajitas)

2 lbs. *fajitas*
1   *onion diced*
1   *bell pepper diced*
1   *tomato diced*
8   *slices of bacon diced*
       Monterrey Jack cheese
12   *flour tortillas*

1. Prepare fajitas as desired, cooking them until medium rare doneness. Slice against the grain and then with the grain chopping into squares.

2. In a skillet cook bacon until done and remove, leaving about 2 tbsp of bacon fat in the skillet. Mix in onions, tomato, and bell pepper; sauté until soft. Mix in cooked bacon and chopped fajitas. Add about 1/4 cup water, stirring often until fajitas are completely cooked.

3. Prepare tortillas or use store bought flour tortillas. On a hot griddle place tortillas with two slices of Monterrey Jack cheese, fold and heat until cheese is partially melted.

4. To serve open tortillas with melted cheese and spoon in fajita mixture and fold the tortilla again.

5. Great party pleasers. They can be prepared before and warmed in the oven.

6. Makes 6 servings.

CHILE RELLENO DE FAJITA (Stuffed Peppers)

4 to 5 *chiles poblano*
4 *eggs separated*
3 tsp. *salt*
2 cups *flour*
2 cups *cooking oil*
fajitas

1. Prepare fajitas ranchero. Set aside.

2. Wash chiles and dry with a towel. Place chiles on a hot griddle turning until blistered on all sides; wrap chiles in a paper towel until cooled. This will soften the skin, so that it can be easily peeled off.

3. Peel skin off chile and slice an opening to remove seeds. (Leave seeds in if you like it Hot!!) Stuff chile with fajita mixture and pin closed with a toothpick.

4. Beat egg whites until fluffy (just like a meringue) and soft peaks are formed. Add egg yolks and salt; beat until thick and fluffy.

5. In a 12 inch skillet heat oil to 370F over medium heat. Roll stuffed Chile in flour, dip into egg mixture and place into hot oil. Fry until golden brown on each side turning with tongs. Drain on paper towel.

6. Makes 4 to 5 servings.

QUESADILLAS DE FAJITAS (Tortillas layered with Fajitas and Cheese)

2 lbs.	fajitas
8	flour tortillas
3 cups	shredded Monterrey Jack cheese
1	onion chopped
1	tomato chopped
1	celery stalk chopped
1	bell pepper chopped
2	cilantro sprigs chopped
$1/2$	chile serrano chopped
$1/2$ tsp	oregano
$1/2$ tsp	comino
$1/2$ tsp	garlic powder
$1/2$ tsp	salt
$1/2$ cup	water

1. Prepare fajitas and chop finely. Prepare tortillas or use store bought. Set aside.

2. In a skillet using 1 tbsp cooking oil saute onions, tomato, celery, bell pepper, cilantro, and chile serrano. Add water and spices to taste. Cook until mixture comes to a boil. Set aside.

3. On an ovenproof serving dish, place tortilla flat on the bottom of the dish; sprinkle generously with cheese. Spread fajita meat on top of cheese. Cover with another tortilla and top with more cheese. Place in the oven at 350F for about 5 minutes or until cheese is melted.

4. Cover tortilla with prepared salsa and serve.

5. Makes 4 servings.

CHICKEN FAJITAS

6	boned chicken breasts
1/2 cup	lemon juice
3 tbsp.	salad oil
3 tbsp.	wine vinegar
1/2 tsp.	salt
1/2 tsp.	pepper
1 tsp.	garlic powder

Boning a chicken breast

1. With a sharp knife working with one side of the breast, starting parallel and close to the large end of the rib cage, cut and scrape meat away from the bone and rib cage, gently pulling back meat in one piece as you cut. Repeat with remaining side. Remove skin and cut out white tendon.

Chicken Marinade

1. Sprinkle salt, pepper and garlic powder evenly over chicken. Mix in lemon juice, oil and vinegar, completely coating chicken. Marinate for 1 hour.

Chicken Fajitas

1. Grill chicken for about 15 minutes or until white. For best results and flavor cook over mesquite.

2. Serve with beef fajitas as a combination and your favorite accompaniment.

3. Makes 6 servings.

FAJITAS KABOB

4 lbs. Fajitas
2 bell peppers cubed
2 onions cubed
1 8 oz. can of cubed pineapple
Fajita Kabob Marinade
Skewers

1. Leave fajitas whole, trimming excess fat and cutting into bite size chunks. Prepare Fajita Kabob Marinade.

2. Mix onions, bell peppers, pineapple and fajitas well into marinade. Cover and refrigerate, stirring mixture often.

3. Prepare grill 30 minutes before cooking. Try this over an open mesquite fire.

4. Thread meat, onion, bell pepper, and pineapple alternately onto 12 inch skewers.

5. Grill for 15 minutes turning skewers or until desired doneness.

6. Makes 6 to 8 servings.

TACOS AL CARBON

3 lbs. Fajitas
12 Flour tortillas

1. Prepare and cook fajitas as desired. Slice fajitas into strips against the grain.

2. Prepare tortillas or use store bought tortillas. Heat on a griddle and wrap in aluminum foil to keep warm.

3. Prepare Guacamole and Salsa. (See pages 18 & 20)

4. Have it buffet style or serve sliced meat in warmed tortillas. Spoon in Guacamole, Salsa and sour cream.

5. Serve with Frijoles A La Charra. (See page 34)

6. Makes 6 servings.

ACCOMPANIMENTS

FRIJOLES (Beans in a Pot)

2 cups pinto beans
5   slices of bacon
1 tsp. garlic salt
1   onion, quartered

1. Clean beans and discard any foreign objects.

2. Rinse beans in a large soup pot. Fill pot with water; add
   beans, onion, bacon and spices. Cover and cook over moder-
   ately high temperature.

3. Check frequently for water. Do not let the beans dry out.
   Keep adding water as needed. Cook until beans are tender,
   about 1 hour or more.

4. Add 1 tbsp. red chili powder for a spicier flavor, if you like.

FRIJOLES A LA CHARRA (Hot Bean Soup)

6   slices of bacon, chopped
1   onion, chopped
1   tomato, chopped
2   cilantro sprigs, chopped
1 tsp. pepper
1 tsp. comino
1   chile, chopped (serrano or jalapeno)

1. Prepare beans in a pot. Set aside.

2. In a skillet cook bacon until done; remove bacon leaving
   about 2 tbsp. of fat in the skillet. Mix in onion, tomato, cilantro, chile and spices. Sauté until soft. Add 1/2 cup of water
   from the beans and bring to a boil.

3. Add salsa to cooked beans and simmer for 30 more minutes.

4. Make FRIJOLES BORRACHOS by adding one can of beer.

5. Serve with warm tortillas or Mexican corn bread.

FRIJOLES REFRITOS   (Refried Beans)

1 tbsp.   bacon drippings
2¹/₂ cups   cooked beans

1. Heat bacon drippings in a skillet; mix in cooked beans and mash completely. Stir beans until they do not stick to the skillet. Cook at a moderate temperature.

2. You can also put cooked beans into a blender and mash; then cook with bacon fat until they are dry and do not stick to the skillet.

FRIJOLES REFRITOS Y QUESO   (Refried Beans & Cheese)

1. After beans have been completely mashed, add slices of Monterrey Jack cheese and cover until cheese is melted.

FRIJOLES REFRITOS A LA RANCHERA   (Refried Beans Ranch Style)

1. Prepare salsa for Frijoles a la Charra. Mix in cooked beans and mash.

2. Make tacos with flour tortillas and serve as an appetizer.

FRIJOLES REFRITOS DE BOTE   (Canned Refried Beans)

1. Heat canned refried beans with bacon drippings, stirring until moist and hot. Add a little salsa or cheese and they'll taste just like homemade beans.

ARROZ MEXICANO   (Mexican Rice)

2 cups   long grain rice
1 can   8 oz. can of tomato sauce
4 cups   water
1 tsp.   garlic powder
1 tsp.   salt
1 tsp.   pepper
dash   comino
1/2   onion, chopped
1/2   bell pepper, chopped
1/4 cup   cooking oil

1. In a skillet brown rice thoroughly in cooking oil. When rice is
    brown mix in bell pepper and onion. Sauté well. Add water,
    tomato sauce and spices.

2. Let rice come to a boil; cover and simmer at a moderate tem-
    perature for about 15 to 20 minutes or until water is gone.

3. Makes 8 servings.

GRILLED ONION

4 whole onions
2 lemons sliced in half
   salt to taste

1. Wash onions and wrap in aluminum foil. Place onion on the
    grill and cook for 30 minutes or until onion is soft.

2. To serve, remove onion from aluminum foil and peel skin
    away. Add lemon juice and salt to taste.

FIDEO MEXICANO (Mexican Vermicelli)

1 5 oz.	box of vermicelli
1 can	tomato sauce
2 cups	water
1/2 tsp.	garlic powder
1/2 tsp.	salt
1/2 tsp.	pepper
dash	comino
1/2	onion, chopped
1/2	bell pepper, chopped
3 tbsp.	cooking oil

1. In a skillet brown fideo in cooking oil, stirring frequently. The fideo will brown quickly. Add chopped onion and bell pepper. Sauté well. Add water, tomato sauce and spices.

2. Let water come to a boil; cover and let simmer for 8 to 10 minutes.

3. Makes 6 servings.

NOPALITOS (Cactus)

5	cactus sliced
3 tbsp.	chili powder
1/2	onion, chopped
1	tomato, chopped
1/4 tsp.	garlic salt

1. In a skillet heat 3 tbsp. of cooking oil; add cactus and cook for about 5 minutes until soft. Add onion, tomato, chili powder and garlic salt. Cook for about 10 minutes.

2. Makes 4 servings.

MEXICAN STUFFED POTATO

4   potatoes
1/2 tsp. garlic salt
4 tbsp. butter
2   small green chiles, chopped
2   cilantro sprigs, chopped
2 cups   grated cheddar cheese

1. Preheat oven to 400F. Wash and dry potatoes. Wrap potatoes in foil and bake for 45 minutes or until fork tender.

2. Remove potatoes from foil and cut in half. Remove potato from the skin and mash. Do not discard skins.

3. Combine garlic salt, butter, green chile, cilantro and cheese into potato and mix well. Return mixture to potato skins. Sprinkle more cheese on top and bake for 15 minutes.

4. Makes 8 servings.

GUACAMOLE   (Avocado Dip)

2   ripe avocados
1/4 cup sour cream
1/2   tomato, chopped finely
1/2   onion, grated
1/2 tsp. garlic salt
2 tbsp. lemon juice

1. Peel avocados and mash well. Add sour cream, tomato, onion, garlic salt and lemon juice; mix well.

2. Garnish with sprinkles of paprika.

CHILE CON QUESO (Chili with Cheese Dip)

1 box   Velveeta cheese
1 8 oz.   can of pet milk
1 10 oz.   can of Rotel tomatoes and green chiles.

1. Using a double boiler at medium temperature, combine cheese and milk; stir until cheese is well melted.

2. Add can of tomatoes and chiles and mix well. For hotter cheese dip add 1 diced jalapeno pepper.

3. As cheese cools it thickens. Serve as a dip or pour over your favorite dish.

APERITIVO DE FRIJOLES (Bean Dip Appetizer)

2 cups   cooked pinto beans
    or
1 can   refried beans
2 tbsp.   sour cream
2 tsp.   garlic powder
2   jalapeno peppers, chopped
4 tbsp.   cooking oil
1 cup   shredded cheddar cheese

1. Heat oil in a skillet and add beans, jalapenos and spices. Mash beans well; simmer until beans do not stick to pan. Spoon bean mixture into serving dish and mix in sour cream.

2. Garnish with shredded cheddar cheese.

PICO DE GALLO   (Rooster's Bill—Cold Salsa)

1 tomato, chopped
1 onion, chopped
5 cilantro sprigs, chopped
1 jalapeno pepper, chopped
1 lemon, cut in half
  salt to taste

1. Mix tomato, onion, cilantro and chile in a serving dish.
   Squeeze lemon juice over mixture and add salt to taste
   and serve.

SALSA

1   onion, chopped
1   tomato, chopped
1   chile pepper, chopped
1 tsp.   garlic salt
1/2 cup   water
1 tbsp.   cooking oil

1. In a skillet sauté onions, tomato and chile in cooking oil until
   soft. Add water and spices. Bring to a boil.

2. If you don't like it hot, replace the chile pepper with black
   pepper to taste.

3. Serve with fajitas or this also makes a great breakfast salsa.

SALSA DE QUESO   (Salsa with Cheese)

Monterrey Jack cheese

1. Repeat step one of the salsa recipe and add cheese after water
   and spices; simmer until cheese is melted.

38

SALSA VERDE (Green Chile Salsa)

8	*tomatillos*
2 tsp	*chile peppers (serrano or jalapeno)*
2 tsp	*garlic powder*
1 tsp	*salt*
1	*large avocado*
½ cup	*milk*

1. Remove leafy skin from tomatillos and boil until soft, about 20 to 30 minutes. Remove and set aside.

2. Boil about 6 chile peppers until soft; about 20 or 30 minutes. Place chiles into blender and blend well; remove and pour into a refrigerated storing container. The blended chile can be frozen and defrosted many times.

3. Blend tomatillo, avocado, 2 tbsp of blended chile, salt, garlic, milk and cilantro until well mixed.

4. This salsa can be served warm or chilled. Keep refrigerated until needed. Mix well before serving.

SALSA ROJA (Red Chile Salsa)

6	*tomatoes*
2 tbsp	*blended chiles (See step 2 of Salsa Verde)*
1 tsp	*salt*
2 tbsp	*garlic powder*

1. Boil tomatoes about 20 minutes until soft. Skin will appear wrinkled. Dip into cold water and slip skin off.

2. Blend tomatoes, chiles, salt and garlic powder; until well mixed.

3. Serve chilled or warm. Keep refrigerated until needed. Stir before serving.

4. Serve as a dip or over your favorite dish.

NOTAS

BREADS/TORTILLAS

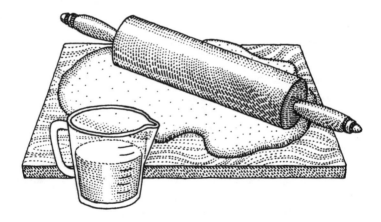

TORTILLAS

Tortillas are sold in most super markets and can be found in the cooler sections of the store; sometimes they have their own special shelf. If you are purchasing pre made tortillas, make sure they are fresh by bending the package back and forth, checking for tenderness and flexibility. These tortillas will need to be reheated or fried before serving.

Many stores also carry pre-mixed tortilla flour; all you need to do is add water and knead, according to directions.

But fresh tortillas are always a winner.

FLOUR TORTILLAS

5 cups	flour
3 tsp	salt
2 tsp	baking powder
¾ cup	shortening
1⅓ cup	warm to hot water

1. Mix flour, salt, baking powder. Knead in shortening until mixture becomes grainy. Add water a little at a time, kneading dough to form a ball. Cover with a towel and let stand for 15 minutes.

2. Preheat ungreased griddle to medium temperature.

3. Break off pieces of dough to form small balls. Flatten balls to biscuit size. With a rolling pin start rolling from center out, forming circle of about 6 to 8 inches in diameter, on a lightly floured surface. Turn tortilla as you roll, stretching as you peel it up.

4. Lay tortilla flat on hot griddle.

5. Cook tortillas almost as pancakes, until they blister on the uncooked side. Turn tortilla over with spatula. Tortillas usually take about 20 to 30 seconds on each side to cook. If the tortilla is cooking too fast or burning, turn the fire down.

6. Makes 18 tortillas.

Corn tortillas are easier bought than they are made and just as good. They can be bought alongside the flour tortillas in most super markets.

Although fresh homemade corn tortillas are absolutely divine.

CORN TORTILLAS

2 cups   Masa Harina (Tortilla corn meal mix)
1⅓ cup   warm water

1. Pour tortilla flour into mixing bowl, adding water a little at a time, and knead into a ball. The dough will be moister than the flour tortilla dough. Divide dough into small balls and flatten with the palm of your hand.

2. Place the ball between two square pieces of waxed paper. Flatten with tortilla press to about 5 to 6 inches in diameter. If a tortilla press is unavailable, flatten the dough with a pie plate.

3. Preheat ungreased griddle. Peel off top layer of waxed paper and place tortilla on griddle, peeling off bottom layer of waxed paper.

4. Cook for about 20 seconds on each side or until edges appear dry and tortilla bubbles.

5. Makes 12 tortillas.

TOSTADAS

Heat ½ cup cooking oil or shortening at medium temperature. Using tongs set tortilla into hot oil and fry for about 1 minute on each side. Some tortillas will bubbleup; to prevent bubbling hold them down with a spatula. Drain them on a paper towel.

TACOS

Heat ½ cup cooking oil or shortening at medium temperature. Using tongs and a fork, set tortilla in oil and fold with the fork until it creases then turn over. Drain on paper towel.

TORTILLA CHIPS

Cut tortilla into squares. Using ½ cup cooking oil or shortening fry a few chips at a time until they are brown and crispy, turning occasionally. Drain on paper towel.

MEXICAN SPOON BREAD

1	8oz. corn muffin mix
1	8oz. creamed corn
1	8oz. whole kernel corn (drained)
1/4 cup	melted butter
1 cup	cottage cheese
2	eggs beaten
1/2 cup	diced green chiles
	Velveeta cheese

1. Preheat oven to 400F

2. In a large bowl, with a fork, combine all of the ingredients, one at a time, mixing well.

3. Stir until mixture is moistened and quickly pour batter into an 8" by 8" baking pan.

4. Spread batter evenly and bake for 40 minutes or until golden brown. Check doneness with a toothpick.

5. Put slices of Velveeta cheese on top of the bread and bake for 5 minutes or until cheese is melted. Spread evenly.

6. Spoon serving onto plate.

NOTAS

DESSERTS & DRINKS

BUNUELOS (Fried Sweet Tortillas)

4 cups   flour
2 tbsp.   shortening
1 tsp.   salt
2 cups   cinnamon tea
4 cups   cooking oil
1 cup   sugar
3 tsp.   cinnamon
3 tbsp.   Mexican chocolate

1. In a mixing bowl, combine flour, shortening and salt. Add cinnamon tea and knead to form a soft dough.

2. Divide into small balls (about the size of golf balls) and roll out to very thin tortillas.

3. In a 12 inch skillet, heat oil to 300F. Fry tortillas until golden brown. Use tong for turning. Tortillas will bubble while frying. Drain on paper towel.

4. Sprinkle a mixture of the sugar, cinnamon and chocolate on each tortilla.

FLAN DE QUESO   (Cheese Custard)

6   *eggs*
1   *8oz. Philadelphia cream cheese*
1   *14oz. Eagle brand milk*
1   *12oz. evaporated milk*
1 cup *sugar*
       custard molds

1. In a medium saucepan over high flame, melt sugar. Lower flame, mixing constantly until golden brown. Quickly pour into custard cup molds.

2. Soften cream cheese until smooth. Add eagle brand milk a small portion at a time, mixing well. Add evaporated milk, mixing slowly and blending well. Add eggs one at a time. Mix well.

3. Pour cheese mixture into molds. Place molds in a large pan in about an inch of water or more. Bake at 300F for 15 minutes, then at 325F for 45 minutes until toothpick inserted in the middle comes out clean.

4. To serve loosen custard with a knife and place in dessert dishes. Refrigerate until served.

BUDIN DE ARROZ   (Rice Pudding)

1 cup   *white rice*
6 cups *water*
5   *cinnamon sticks*
2 cups *sugar*
1 8oz. *can of evaporated milk*

1. In a saucepan boil cinnamon sticks in 6 to 8 cups of water; add sugar and cook until it comes to a full boil.

2. Strain tea, removing cinnamon sticks. In a saucepan; add 1 cup of rice and 6 cups of cinnamon tea; stirring frequently until mixture comes to a boil.

3. Reduce heat to low; cover and simmer for 30 minutes or until rice is very tender. Stir in milk and mix well. Cover and let mixture stand for 20 minutes.

4. Serve chilled or warm with a sprinkle of cinnamon on top.

EMPANADAS DE CERVEZA   (Sweet Beer Turnovers)

4 cups   *flour*
1/2 cup *shortening*
1 can   *beer at room temperature*
1 cup   *sugar*
2 tsp.   *cinnamon*

1. In a large mixing bowl, combine flour and shortening, mixing well. Add beer a little at a time to form a soft dough.

2. Make balls of dough and roll out to size desired.

3. Fill with pie filling desired. Fold dough over and close edges, crimping with a wet fork.

4. Place empanadas on a greased cookie sheet and bake at 400F for 30 minutes or until golden brown.

5. Mix 1 cup sugar and 2 tsp. cinnamon and set aside.

6. Remove empanadas from the oven and roll in sugar and cinnamon mixture.

CAPIROTADA (Bread Pudding)

1	loaf of white bread toasted
1 lb	Longhorn cheddar cheese; shredded
1 cup	raisins
1 cup	pecans, chopped
1 cup	dark brown sugar
4 cups	cinnamon tea
8	cinnamon sticks
1½ cup	sugar

1. In saucepan boil cinnamon sticks in 6-8 cups of water; add sugar and bring to a full boil.

2. Strain tea removing cinnamon sticks. Soak raisins and chopped pecans in 3 cups of cinnamon tea.

3. In a casserole dish, layer toast, cheese, mixture of raisins and pecans and brown sugar. Pour remaining cup of cinnamon tea over filled casserole. Bread should be very moist.

4. Bake at 350F for about 35 minutes.

SOPAPILLAS (Fried Bisquit Puffs)

1 pkg.	refrigerated biscuit dough
1 cup	cooking oil
	honey

1. Heat oil in a skillet. Spread single biscuits out with your fingers and press the biscuits almost flat. Drop into hot oil, until golden brown on both sides. Drain on a paper towel.

2. Serve warm with a spoon full of natural honey.

MARGARITA

11 oz. lime juice
3 oz. tequila
3 oz. triple sec

1. Mix all ingredients. Pour over ice.

2. For frozen Margaritas, mix in blender with ice.

3. Prepare glasses by rubbing the edge of the glass with lime juice and dip the edge of the glass in a salt-filled plate.

PINA COLADA

2 oz. rum
1 oz. Creme de Cocoa
3 oz. pineapple juice
       ice

1. Mix all ingredients in a blender until ice is well crushed. Pour into glass and garnish with a fresh slice of pineapple.

SANGRIA

1/2 cup sugar
1 cup   orange juice, concentrate
1 fifth red wine
1 fifth white wine
1/4 cup brandy
1   lemon wedge

1. Combine ingredients and mix well. Refrigerate and serve chilled over ice.

NOTAS

NOTAS

GLOSSARY/INDEX

Glossary

TOMATILLOS: Little green tomatoes with a paper like skin that is peeled off before cooking. Tart in flavor and are mostly used in making salsas. They are usually boiled until softened and blended with other ingredients for the salsa. They can be found in the produce section of your grocery store and also canned.

NOPALITOS: (Cactus) These young tender buds of the Prickly Pear cactus are served as vegetables. They are oval shaped and can be found in the produce section whole or packaged already cut. The thorns are scraped from the pads and are not peeled. The cactus can also be found canned.

CILANTRO: (Coriander) This fresh leafy seasoning resembles parsley only in appearance not in taste. You can smell the tangy flavor the cilantro has. They can be found in the produce section of the grocery store.

CHILI POWDER: Can be found with the spices in most grocery stores. Chili powder consists of ground dried red chiles and a mixture of cumin, oregano and garlic.

CHILE POBLANO: Is a large bell pepper like chile, only pointed and curved rather than square. The poblano chile can be mild to hot in taste. It is usually stuffed, but can be dried and crushed into chili powder.

CHILE JALAPENO: Is a dark green pepper with a thicker flesh and about 2 to 3 inches long. The jalapeno chile is extremely hot and can be found fresh or canned.

CHILE SERRANO: Is a green to red colored pepper, much thinner than the jalapeno chile and are about 1 inch long. The serrano pepper is also extremely hot and can be found fresh or canned.